NOTE TO PARENTS

Welcome to Kingfisher Readers! This program is designed to help young readers build skills, confidence, and a love of reading as they explore their favorite topics.

These tips can help you get more from the experience of reading books together. But remember, the most important thing is to make reading fun!

Tips to Warm Up Before Reading

- Look through the book with your child. Ask them what they notice about the pictures.
- Wonder aloud together. Ask questions and make predictions. What will this book be about? What are some words we could expect to find on these pages?

While Reading

- Take turns or read together until your child takes over.
- Point to the words as you say them.
- When your child gets stuck on a word, ask if the picture could help. Then think about the first letter too.
- Accept and praise your child's contributions.

After Reading

- Look back at the things your child found interesting. Encourage connections to other things you both know.
- Draw pictures or make models to explore these ideas.
- Read the book again soon, to build fluency.

With five distinct levels and a wealth of appealing topics, the Kingfisher Readers series provides children with an exciting way to learn to read and wonder about the world around them. Enjoy!

Ellie Costa, M.S. Ed.
Literacy Specialist, Bank Street School for Children, New York

KINGFISHER READERS

level 1

Butterflies

Thea Feldman

KINGFISHER
NEW YORK

KINGFISHER
LONDON & NEW YORK

Distributed in the U.S. and Canada by Macmillan,
175 Fifth Ave., New York, NY 10010

Library of Congress Cataloging-in-Publication data
has been applied for.

Series editor: Thea Feldman
Literacy consultant: Ellie Costa, Bank St. College, New York

ISBN: 978-0-7534-6748-0 (HB)
ISBN: 978-0-7534-6749-7 (PB)

Kingfisher books are available for special promotions
and premiums. For details contact: Special Markets
Department, Macmillan, 175 Fifth Ave.,
New York, NY 10010.

For more information, please visit
www.kingfisherbooks.com

Printed in China
9 8 7 6 5 4 3 2 1
1TR/1011/WKT/UNTD/105MA

Picture credits

The Publisher would like to thank the following for permission to reproduce their material. Every care has been taken to trace copyright holders. However, if there have been unintentional omissions or failure to trace copyright holders, we apologize and will, if informed, endeavor to make corrections in any future edition.
Top = t; Bottom = b; Center = c; Left = l; Right = r
Cover Shutterstock/Kuttelvaserova; Pages 3 Photolibrary/Bios; 3 Shutterstock/Serg64; 4 Photoshot/ NHPA/Jordi Bas Casas; 5 Corbis/Papillo; 6t Photolibrary/Bios; 6b Shutterstock/nodiff; 7cl Frank Lane Picture Agency (FLPA)/Wim Reyns/Minden; 7cr Shutterstock/freepainter; 7bl Photolibrary/Superstock; 7br Corbis/Tim Zurowski/All Canada Photos; 8 Photolibrary/Bios; 9 Shutterstock/SaraJo; 10t Shutterstock/Miles Boyar; 10b Corbis/Darrell Gulin; 11t Shutterstock/Willem Dijkstra; 11b FLPA/ Malcolm Schuyl; 12 Getty/flickr; 13 Photoshot/NHPA/ Jordi Bas Casas; 14 Alamy/Natural History Museum; 15 Alamy/Corbis; 16 Getty/Darrell Gulin; 17 Photolibrary/Imagebroker; 18–19 FLPA/Michael Weber; 19 Shutterstock/Olga Bogatyrenko; 20 Naturepl/Ingo Arndt; 21 Photoshot/NHPA/T. Hitchin & V. Hurst; 22 Photolibrary/OSF; 23 Photolibrary/Animals Animals; 24t FLPA/WaterFrame; 24b Alamy/Don Johnston; 25t Naturepl/Doug Wechsler; 25b Photolibrary/Peter Arnold Images; 26l Photolibrary/ Don Johnston; 26r Alamy/Phil Degginger; 27 Corbis/Skip Moody/Rainbow; 28 Naturepl/Ingo Arndt; 29 Corbis/T. Hitchin & V. Hurst; 30–31 Getty/Iconica; 30–31 Naturepl/Stephen Dalton.

Do you see
something pretty in the air?

It is a **butterfly**!

A butterfly is an **insect**.

Not all insects can fly.

But butterflies do!

Butterflies have wings.

The wings are covered
in tiny scales.

Some butterflies are colorful.

Look at all the colorful butterflies!

Birds, snakes, and other animals eat butterflies.

But colorful butterflies can stay safe.

A colorful butterfly may
taste bad.

It may have poison in its body.

Its colors warn other animals
not to eat it.

How else do butterflies
stay safe?

Some butterflies have big spots
on their wings.

The spots look like big,
scary eyes!

The spots keep hungry
animals away.

This is a **moth**.

Moths and butterflies
look a lot alike.

But they are different.

One way they are different
is that moths fly at night.

Butterflies fly in the daytime.

This is the biggest butterfly.
It is bigger than this book.

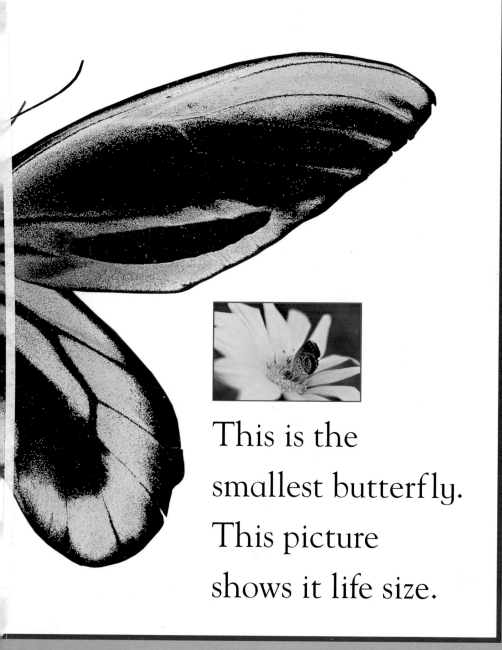

This is the
smallest butterfly.
This picture
shows it life size.

Butterflies look for flowers.

They drink **nectar** from flowers.

Slurp!

A butterfly's tongue is like
a drinking straw.

How can a butterfly tell
if a flower tastes good?

It uses its feet!

A butterfly's **taste buds** are on its feet.

Where are your taste buds?

A butterfly lays eggs on leaves.

The eggs will hatch
by themselves.

Surprise!

Look who comes out.
A **caterpillar**!

A caterpillar does not look like
a butterfly.

But a caterpillar is
a baby butterfly.

Munch, munch, munch.

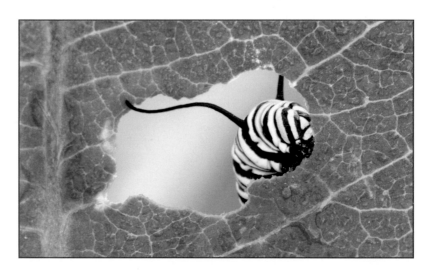

The caterpillar eats and eats.

It eats leaves.

The caterpillar grows and grows.

One day the caterpillar
stops eating.

It makes a safe place to stay.

The safe place is called
a **chrysalis**.

It stays inside the chrysalis
for a few weeks.

27

Surprise!

Look who comes out.

The caterpillar
is now a butterfly!

Do you see something pretty in the air?

It is a butterfly, all grown up!

Glossary

butterfly a type of insect that flies in the daytime

caterpillar a baby butterfly

chrysalis a place a caterpillar makes that keeps it safe for a few weeks while it turns into a butterfly

insect a type of small animal with six legs

moth a type of insect that flies at night

nectar a sweet juice found in flowers that butterflies drink with their tongues

taste buds tiny parts of the body that can tell what something tastes like. People have taste buds on the tongue. Butterflies have taste buds on the feet.

If you have enjoyed reading this book, look out for more in the Kingfisher Readers series!

KINGFISHER READERS: LEVEL 1

Baby Animals
Butterflies
Colorful Coral Reefs
Jobs People Do
Snakes Alive!
Trains

KINGFISHER READERS: LEVEL 2

What Animals Eat
Your Body

KINGFISHER READERS: LEVEL 3

Dinosaur World
Volcanoes

KINGFISHER READERS: LEVEL 4

Pirates
Weather

KINGFISHER READERS: LEVEL 5

Ancient Egyptians
Rainforests

For a full list of Kingfisher Readers books, plus guidance for teachers and parents and activities and fun stuff for kids, go to the Kingfisher Readers website: **www.kingfisherreaders.com**